SCIENCE
MUSEUM

THIS BOOK THINKS YOU'RE AN INVENTOR

EXPERIMENT
IMAGINE
CREATE

FILL-IN PAGES FOR YOUR IDEAS

ILLUSTRATED BY HARRIET RUSSELL

Thames & Hudson

T0275537

Produced in association with **SCIENCE MUSEUM** ® SCMG

This Book Thinks You're an Inventor © 2020 Thames and Hudson Ltd, London
Illustrations © 2020 Harriet Russell

Text by Georgia Amson-Bradshaw
Designed by Belinda Webster
With special thanks to Jon Milton

First published in 2020 in the United States of America by Thames & Hudson Inc.,
500 Fifth Avenue, New York, New York 10110

www.thamesandhudsonusa.com

Library of Congress Control Number 2019931892

ISBN 978-0-500-65176-6

Printed and bound in China by C & C Offset Printing Co. Ltd

Photography credits:
All photographs © Science Museum/Science & Society Picture Library

THIS BOOK THINKS YOU'RE AN INVENTOR

ILLUSTRATED BY HARRIET RUSSELL

The world needs INVENTORS. Without them, we wouldn't have such amazing and essential things as karaoke machines or scented erasers. (Plus some other stuff such as computers or antibiotics, or whatever).

ANYONE CAN BE AN INVENTOR. You just have to think of something—literally anything—and then think of a way it could be better. For example, how could an umbrella be better?

This book thinks YOU are an inventor, so come on, get started on the next big thing...

CONTENTS

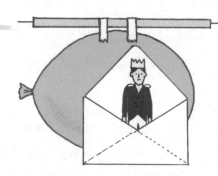

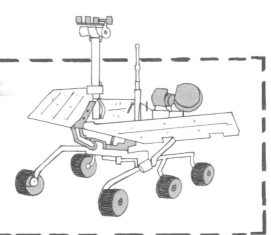

DISCOVER YOUR INVENTING STYLE

DO THIS!

There isn't one right way to be an inventor.
Follow this quiz to find out your inventing style.

Are you always taking things apart to see how they work?

yes →

Which is the better birthday present—a multi-tool or a sketchbook?

→ **multi-tool**

↓ **no**

↓ **sketchbook**

→ **rocket**

Do you daydream about worlds, or play imaginative games about aliens, robots and spaceships?

no →

What would make you more proud—inventing the world's fastest ever rocket, or inventing a pair of angel-style wings that people could use to fly?

→ **wings**

↓ **yes**

no ↗

Do people sometimes say your ideas are silly or not possible?

→ **math**

yes →

Which subject do you prefer: art or math?

art

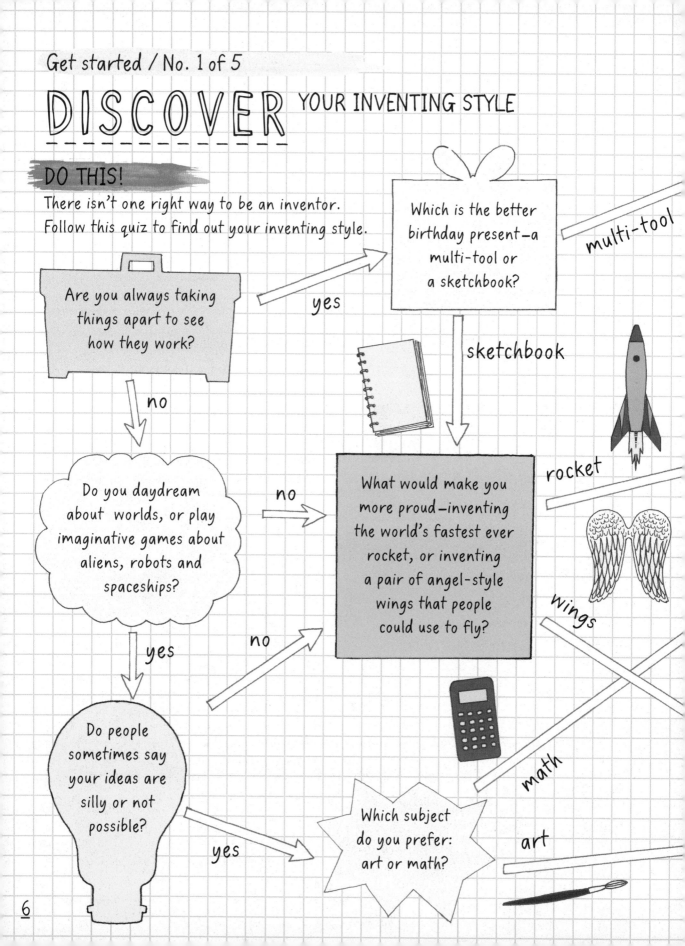

Do you read instruction manuals or do you learn how things work by trial and error?

trial and error →

read manual

make do

You are a DOER!
A practical and hands-on person, your favorite hobby is to make things. Designing is fun, but really you just want to get on with making your inventions to see if they actually work. The Wright brothers, who managed the first controlled airplane flight, were doers. They worked for years in a workshop with bicycles, motors and other machines, gaining practical skills and learning as they went.

You are a REFINER!
For you, perfection is the name of the game. You are very clear-sighted and can immediately see a dozen different ways to improve an object. This sort of perfectionism is what wins the day in sports engineering, where racing bikes need to be made lighter, or swimsuits sleeker so that athletes can perform even better.

Does it really annoy you if something you own doesn't work perfectly, or are you happy to make do?

get annoyed →

factual ↑

You are a DREAMER!
Your inventing style is to dream big. You are very creative and you like coming up with amazing new never-been-seen-before ideas, even if you're not quite sure how they'll work! By thinking outside the box, dreamers like you really push things forward. Leonardo da Vinci was a famous dreamer who imagined a rotor-helicopter hundreds of years before it was successfully built.

What sort of TV programs do you like better: factual and documentary, or fantasy and sci-fi dramas?

drama

HATE SOMETHING, CHANGE SOMETHING

DO THIS!

Think of some problems that are small but annoying. For example:

Are your parents' house keys always going missing?

Do your parents always make you pick up stuff from your bedroom floor?

Does your dog bark loudly all the time?

Ask yourself: what could you invent to solve these problems? Perhaps you could...

Invent a keyring with wheels that rolls in your direction when you whistle?

Invent a vacuum that comes out of the ceiling and can vacuum up all the mess.

Invent a digital muzzle that converts dog barks into beautiful singing.

OK, maybe those aren't the most sensible suggestions. Can you come up with better solutions to some common annoying problems? Draw them below.

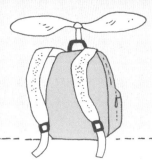

This invention is called:................................

....

It solves the problem of:.............................

....

This invention is called:................................

....

It solves the problem of:.............................

....

INGENIOUS INVENTIONS

Tin cans were being used for preserving food as early as 1772. Unfortunately, the can opener had not been invented! People had to figure out how to open their cans using hammers, chisels and whatever other tools they had lying around. Which is fine, if you want your food mashed up or all over the floor. It wasn't until 1855 that Robert Yeates from Middlesex, UK, invented a claw shaped can opener.

FILL YOUR INVENTING TOOLBOX

Quick question for you:
what are these?

If you said "they're just rocks,"
I'm afraid you are WRONG!
They are tools that are 3.3 million
years old. They were made by our
ancestors, before humans even existed!

This is Lucy, she is from the early human species called
Australopithecus afarensis. This type of ancient primate might
have made those stone tools.

This tool is incredibly
versatile. I use it for
gardening, cooking,
even walking the dog.

Those ancient stone tools could only really cut or hammer things.
Nowadays, we have tools for doing all sorts of things.

DO THIS!

Look again at the things you invented on the previous page. What tools might you need to make them? Draw those tools in the toolbox below. But first, will you do it the easy way or the hard way?

 easy mode
Search online for possible tools. For example, what tools and machines are used to shape plastic? Or to cut metal?

super hard mode
Try to invent the tools yourself. Think about what materials your invention would be made of and what tools you'd need to shape them.

MY TOOLBOX

SPIN THE WHEEL OF INVENTION

DO THIS!

1st

Go to page 62 and cut out the wheel of invention. Poke a pencil through the middle of the circle to turn it into a spinner.

2nd

Spin your spinner twice, or if you're feeling really clever, three times. Note the picture that it lands on each time.

3rd

Now invent something that uses each of the objects your spinner landed on. For example, if it landed on a hat and a rope, you could invent a hat that is made of a single piece of rope zipped up in a spiral, which unzips back into a rope!

Note down your spinner pictures here, and jot down some invention ideas.

When you have an idea you are happy with, draw and label it in detail in this box.

INGENIOUS INVENTIONS

Nowadays many of us carry around a
device that combines hundreds of separate
inventions in one. Can you think what it
is? A smartphone! This single object is
a phone, music player, map, camera,
alarm clock, calendar, photo album,
notebook, game console—and more!

WRECK YOUR TECH

Release your inner monster and DESTROY STUFF!

DO THIS!

1st

Ask your parents if there's a broken appliance that you can take apart, such as an old TV remote, or ancient stereo equipment that no one wants.

How many pieces do you think are inside?
Can any of the parts be recycled?

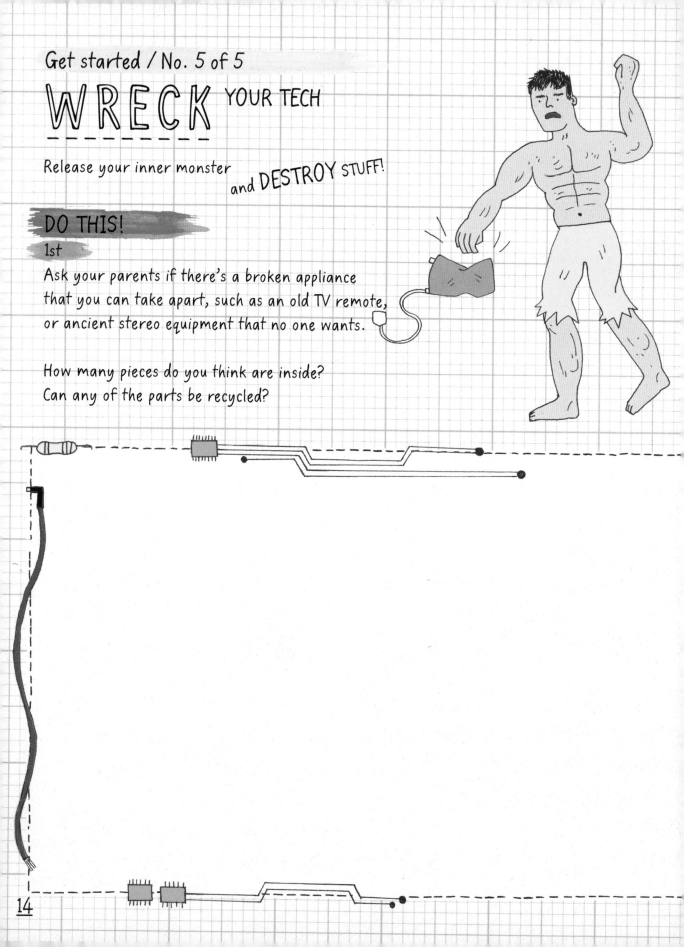

INGENIOUS INVENTIONS

Taking an object apart to see how it is made is actually a real thing that inventors do. It's called "reverse engineering." Companies will often take a competing business's product apart to see how it's made, and make a version of their own!

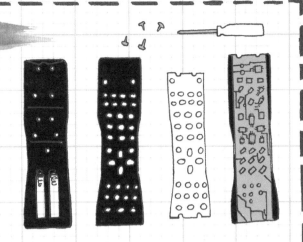

2nd

Carefully take apart your old appliance. Record what you find by drawing each of the pieces in this box.

MEGA WARNING:
Ask permission before taking anything apart and be careful of sharp edges. Don't try to put it back together. DO NOT CUT, PIERCE OR TAKE BATTERIES APART!

HUNT AROUND YOUR HOUSE

Have you ever heard the phrase "as useless as a chocolate teapot?" There's no point coming up with a brilliant idea for an invention then making it out of an unsuitable material, or you'll end up with a lap full of hot tea and chocolate stains on everything. We have to choose materials with the right properties, such as hardness, weight and strength.

GAH!
Not again!

DO THIS!

Look around your house and see how many different materials you can spot.
What are the different types of materials used for?
Why do you think that material has been chosen?

Material ....

What it has been chosen for, and why

....

....

....

Material ....

What it has been chosen for, and why

....

....

....

Material ....

What it has been chosen for, and why

....

....

....

Material ....

What it has been chosen for, and why

....

....

....

INGENIOUS INVENTIONS

People don't just make inventions from materials...
they invent entirely new materials! In 1964 U.S.
chemist Stephanie Kwolek invented Kevlar®, which is the
plastic fiber that bulletproof vests are made of. And in
2004, Andre Geim and Konstantin Novoselov invented
graphene—a material that is a single atom thick and
almost invisible. It's used in bendable mobile phones
and tiny medical robots that go inside your body!

Scientists have recently invented more wonder materials, including:

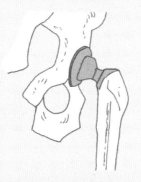

biodegradable plastic
made from shrimp
shells and spider silk

titanium foam that replaces
injured bones, which new
bone will grow around

an edible plastic made from
seaweed that can be used
for drinking straws

DO THIS!

Dream up a new material.
Give it a name and describe
what it's like and what
it can be used for.

FEED THE BIRDS (OR DO SOMETHING ELSE WITH A PLASTIC BOTTLE)

Plastic—it's fantastic! Except for the fact that, around the world, hardly any of it is recycled, and a lot of it ends up as pollution. That's not so fantastic.

The reason plastic is so widely used is because it's light, strong, cheap and it can be used for lots of different purposes.

We should all try to use less plastic, but for the plastic we already have it's important to reuse it before we throw it away.

> Why do we use so much plastic anyway?

DO THIS!

Come up with lots of different ways to upcycle a plastic bottle into another useful item. Here are some examples:

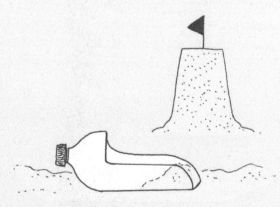

Cut the bottom off, leaving one side longer to make a scoop.

Cut it in half and turn the top into a funnel and the bottom into a plant pot.

Fill it with dry beans to make a musical rattle.

Cut a hole in the side, fill it with seeds and hang it up to make a bird feeder.

Now it's your turn! Draw some plastic bottle inventions here.

INVENT A NEW USE FOR PAPER

You're probably getting the hang of this inventing thing now. You may have noticed that most of the time, inventing is actually just slightly tweaking or coming up with a new use for something that already exists. So can you come up with a new use for paper?

Hmm, perhaps my paper bucket invention needs more thought...

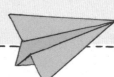

DO THIS!

Come up with a design for a new paper invention here.

Think about the properties of paper—what is it useful for?

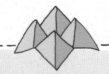

Need some inspiration? How about...

Paper underpants

Ow! I have a paper-cut on my butt!

Hmmm...now why isn't this working?

A paper computer

A paper bicycle

DO THIS!

Turn to page 65 to find some paper that you can use to test your idea and make your invention (or a small model of it).

INGENIOUS INVENTIONS

Paper was invented in China aound 2,000 years ago, and while the ideas above might sound silly, paper is actually a very adaptable material. In the 1960s there was a trend for paper clothing, particularly dresses which could be printed in bright patterns and sold very cheaply. There were even paper wedding dresses and underwear available! However, the clothes were uncomfortable and flammable, so the novelty wore off and they fell out of fashion.

SWEETEN SOME SCIENCE

I love to talk about properties!

Let's talk some more about properties.

Not house properties! The properties of materials, such as how they act when they get wet, or when they are heated and cooled. These sorts of properties are very important when inventing new things.

DO THIS!

Collect several types of sweets, such as a mint, a piece of chocolate, a cookie and a marshmallow. Put each sweet in a separate small bowl or cup, and fill each one with cold water.

After 30 minutes, give them each a stir. Leave them for another 30 minutes. After the full hour, look at them again. How has the texture of each sweet changed? Record the results below.

Sweet type				
Texture of sweet				
Texture of sweet after soaking				

DO THIS!

Find a clean ice cube tray. Fill each section of the tray with a different type of sweet food, for example, honey, chocolate sauce, fruit juice, jam, toast and jelly (use both liquids and solids). Put the tray in the freezer.

Check your ice cube tray three times: after 30 minutes, 1 hour and then leave overnight and check in the morning. Each time, poke the food in the tray. How does the texture of each sweet food change over time? Write your results in the chart below.

Sweet food type and texture				
Texture after 30 minutes				
Texture after 1 hour				
Texture after 12-24 hours				

Now you have finished the experiment, what sweet would you use to...

Build a house in a rainy country?

Fill a kiddie pool at the North Pole?

ENGINEER YOUR 'DO

What do you think engineers do?

Do you think they work with machines, cogs and engines?

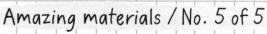

Or maybe you think they work with wires, plugs and electricity?

Well, those things are true, but that's not the whole story. There are all kinds of engineers, from civil engineers who design and build roads, bridges and buildings...

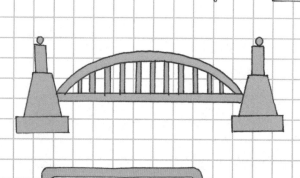

...to information engineers who work with computers, software and robots...

...and textile engineers who make new fabrics, or turn fabrics into new inventions. Medical engineers design medical equipment and artificial body parts and chemical engineers develop new fuels, foods, drugs and more! PHEW!

DO THIS!

Be a textile engineer and use your hair (or someone else's) to make a wacky hair structure. You could:

Create a hair octopus

Make 8 small braids around the head, with a ponytail on top. Wrap pipe cleaners around the braids so they can be bent into wiggly shapes and stuck out from the head. Backcomb the ponytail on top and pin the ends of the hair behind to create the octopus head. Spray with a colorful hairspray and attach googly eyes for the finishing touch.

Engineer a unicorn horn

Take a piece of card and roll it into a cone shape with a hole in the top. Make a small ponytail on the top of your head with half of your hair. Thread it up through the hole in the top of the cone. Wind the ponytail down and around the cone so your hair covers the cone completely. Pin the end of the ponytail to the head. Put the rest of the hair into a ponytail at the back, to be the unicorn's tail.

DO THIS!

Engineer your own hair-dos. Sketch some ideas on these heads:

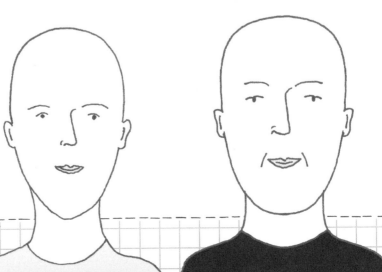

SLIDE LIKE A SNAIL

Humans are naturally talented at a lot of things. However, when it comes to transporting ourselves using only our bodies, we're less impressive. We can't even fly! By comparison, fleas can jump 100 times their own height, peregrine falcons can fly at 242 mph and basilisk lizards can walk on water!

Neat trick!

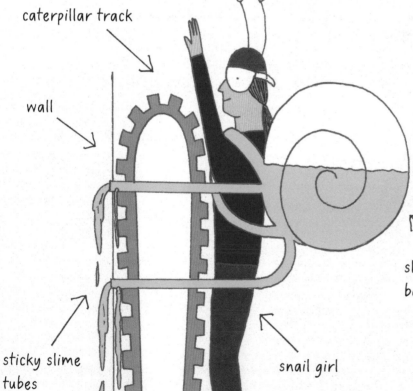

caterpillar track

wall

sticky slime tubes

snail girl

slime tank back pack

DO THIS!

Think of an animal ability that you would like to have. How about sliding up vertical surfaces like a snail? What could you invent to give yourself that ability?

DO THIS!

Draw and label your animal-inspired transport invention here:

INGENIOUS INVENTIONS

"Biomimetics" is the name for inventing things by borrowing ideas from animals and plants. British designer Fiona Fairhurst took inspiration from the texture of a shark's ridged skin, which helps it swim faster, when she invented the fastskin swimsuit. The suit worked so well that it was banned at the Olympics for giving swimmers an unfair advantage.

PING YOUR PRINCE

Oh no! A prince is being chased by a fire-breathing dragon.
He will be safe once he's inside his castle, but the drawbridge
is closed. Can you invent something to rescue him?
You'll need to get the prince across the moat...
and you better be quick, or the dragon might catch you!

DO THIS!

Turn to page 69 and cut out the prince, the tower
and the dragon. Put the dragon and the prince on
one side of a room in your house. Put the tower on
the other side. Now invent a way to get the prince
safely across the room.

Build a balloon monorail

1. Tie a long piece of string to a chair or
   a doorknob on one side of the room.
2. Thread the loose end of the string through
   a drinking straw and tie it to another object
   on the opposite side of the room.
3. Blow up a balloon and hold the opening of
   it between your fingers so no air escapes
   (you might need someone to help with the
   next bit if your hands are full with the balloon).

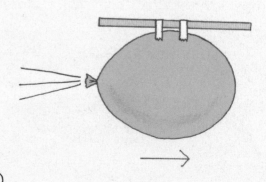

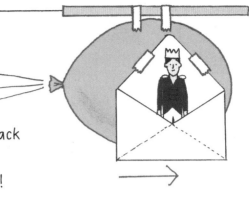

4. Tape the balloon to the straw so that the opening of the balloon points backward.

5. Tape an envelope for the prince to sit in on the side of the balloon. Draw the balloon back to the end of the string closest to the dragon. Release the balloon to let the air escape. Whoosh! Does the prince make it to safety?

Invent a princely catapult

1. Stack 5 popsicle sticks together and wrap a rubber band around each end to make the base.
2. Take 2 more popsicle sticks and wrap a rubber band around just one end to make the catapult.
3. Wedge the base between the two sticks of the catapult.
4. Fix the base to the catapult by looping a big rubber band to cross over the join.
5. Attach a plastic spoon to the top stick of the catapult using more rubber bands.
6. Attach the paper prince to something slightly heavy, such as a small stone.
7. Sit the paper prince in the spoon, and pull the spoon down towards the ground, while holding the prince in place.
8. Let go. Ping!

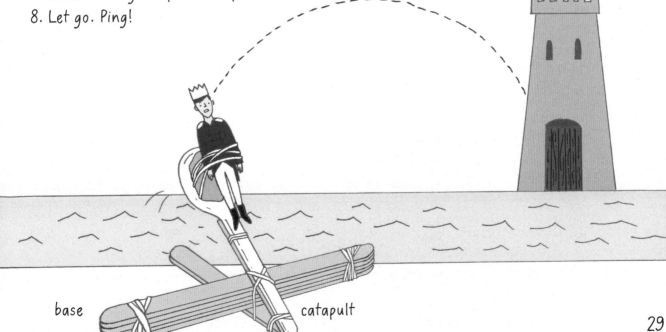

base   catapult

PIMP YOUR RIDE

In the future our cars will drive themselves. If we don't need
to be watching the road and operating the vehicle, we could do
anything inside the car. Instead of forward-facing seats,
you could have a ball pit, or a 3D movie screen...
or whatever you like!

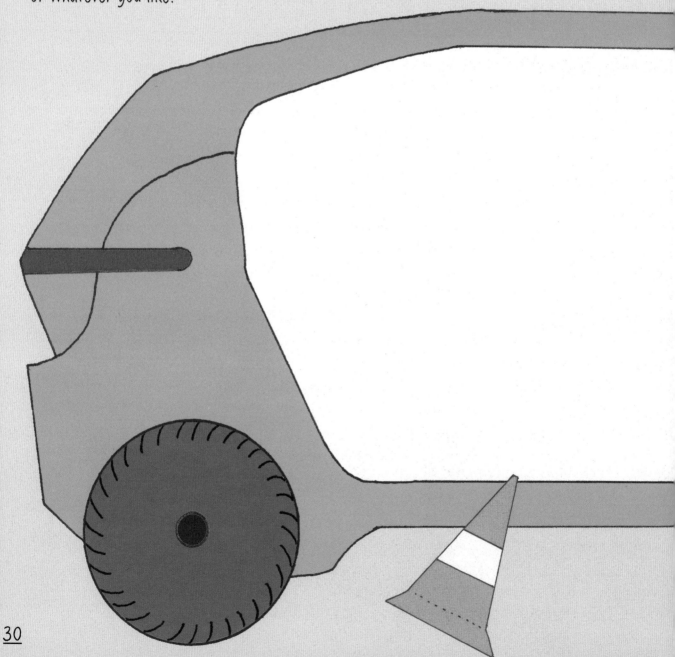

DO THIS!

Draw and label what you'd have inside your driverless car.

Would you have a bed?

Which way would you face?

What screens and controls might you need?

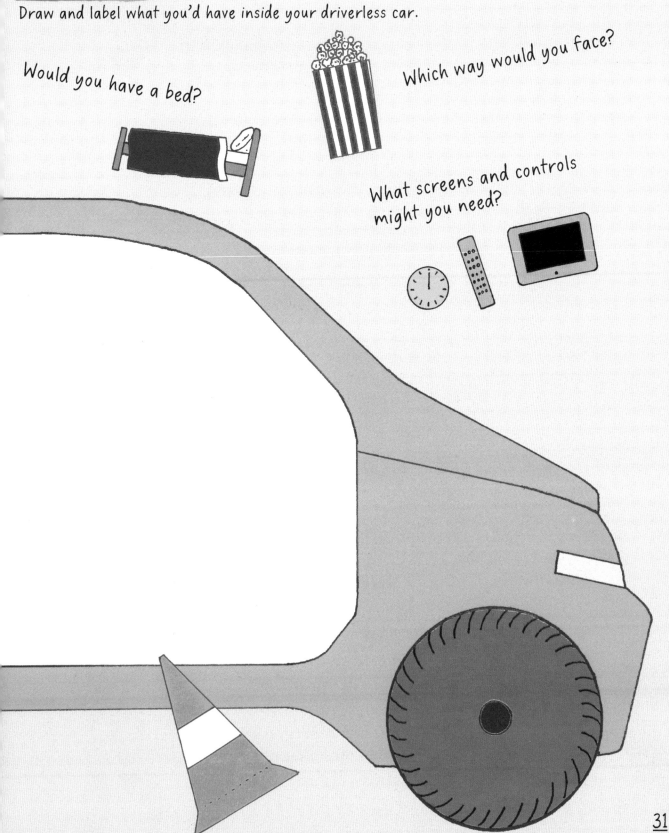

FLY LIKE A BIRD

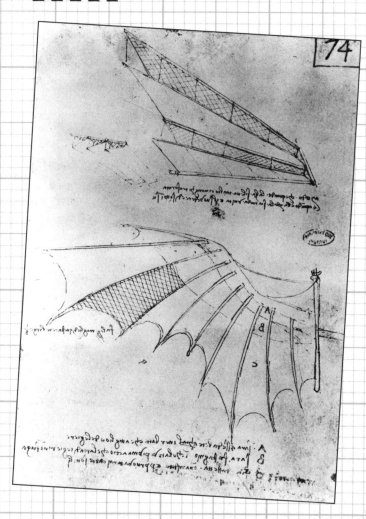

74

When the famous inventor Leonardo da Vinci was a baby, a hawk hovered over his cradle. The story goes that this gave da Vinci the idea to invent all sorts of flying machines inspired by birds.

Unfortunately, the ones he designed had flapping wings that weren't able to lift a human off the ground.

Leonardo da Vinci's designs and diaries were written in code, to keep his ideas secret.

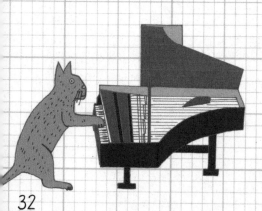

Leonardo also invented an armored, cone-shaped tank inspired by a turtle's shell, a helicopter-like flying machine, a diving suit made from pigskin, a mechanical robot knight operated by pulleys and an instrument called the viola organista that was a cross between a piano and a violin.

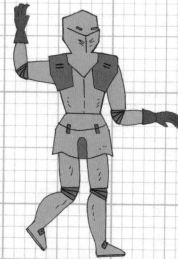

INGENIOUS INVENTIONS

As well as drawing flapping flying machines, Leonardo invented a glider (which would have worked if he had ever tested it). Gliders and planes fly using an airfoil-shaped wing. An airfoil wing is curved at the front and angled downwards at the back.

Air splits into two streams around curved side of airfoil wing

Air travels down along the airfoil wing to the back edge

Plane is lifted up as air is pushed down over the wings

As the wing moves through the sky, it splits the air into two streams. The air above the wing follows the curve. As it leaves the back edge the air is angled downward-this is called "downwash". The downwash pushes the air below the wing downward. By pushing the air downward, the plane is lifted up.

DO THIS!

Draw a new design for a flying machine here. Use an animal as inspiration in combination with what you know about airfoil wings.

Turn to page 71 for fun flying machine crafts.

TURN THIS BOOK INTO A MACHINE

How could you turn this book into a machine? Would you cut it up into individual cogs and gears, and reassemble them as a moving machine?

Or would you add wires and use electricity to move it?

Actually, you don't need to do anything fancy to make this book a machine!

You just need to put it at an angle.

WHAT?

THIS BOOKS THINKS YOU'RE AN INVENTOR

It doesn't look like a machine to me!

The simplest definition of a machine is an instrument used to make forces (pulling and pushing forces) bigger.

RAMP

The simplest machine of all is a ramp. Imagine you have to get a very heavy box up into the back of a truck. Lifting it straight up would be very hard work. But if you had a ramp up to the truck, you could push the box up the slope. It's much easier than lifting the heavy box through the air. But the trade off is that you have to move the box a longer distance along the ramp.

LEVER

Another simple machine is the lever. A lever is a beam that pivots around a fixed point, like a seesaw. But if you move the fixed point closer to one end of the beam, you can reduce the amount of force needed to lift a load off the ground.

DO THIS!
Use your book as a ramp or a lever to move an object.

EAT YOUR DINNER

Which of these objects is a piece of technology?

TRICK QUESTION! They are all technology.
Technology is simply the tools or knowledge that
humans use to solve a problem or make things easier.
For example, the knife is a piece of technology
that makes it easier for humans to cut their food
into smaller pieces and eat it.

DO THIS!

Find a fork or soup spoon.
What else could you use it for? List some alternative uses for it here:

....

....

....

....

....

Around the world, people use different types of technology to eat their food.

In some places, they use chopsticks.

Elsewhere, knives, forks and spoons are used.

In Ethiopia, food is often served on a type of pancake that is torn into bits and used to scoop up food.

DO THIS!

Go around your house and see if you can find things that you could eat with (instead of normal silverware). What shapes and materials would work best?

IMAGINEER FUTURE TECH

Can you identify these pieces of ancient technology?
Answers are on page 96!

A

B

C

D

Those old things look very outdated now, but once upon a time they were brand new and exciting inventions. In the future, some of the new pieces of technology that you use now will also look really ancient.

DO THIS!

An imagineer is someone who comes up with very imaginative new technology. Can you come up with a totally new piece of technology that everyone will want in their home?

INGENIOUS INVENTIONS

A lot of home technology that we now take for granted was invented by women. In 1886, Josephine Cochrane invented the dishwasher. In 1914, Florence Parpart invented the electric refrigerator and in 1919, Alice Parker invented gas-fired central heating.

More recently, Joy Mangano created two hugely popular home items: the self-wringing mop in 1990 and the velvet flocked non-slip clothes hanger in 1999.

BE A CHILD GENIUS

What's your greatest ever achievement? What have you done in your life that you are most proud of?

If the answer is "ummm...nothing," then now is your chance to change all that. Join the hall of fame with these other child inventors:

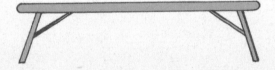

Frank Epperson invented the popsicle at age 11

George Nissen invented the trampoline at age 16

Benjamin Franklin, one of the forefathers of the U.S. invented swim fins at age 11

Kids have invented a lot of fun things including toys, sweet treats and sports equipment that have gone on to be very successful products.

DO THIS!

Invent a new type of sweet, toy or game.
Brainstorm some ideas here.

DO THIS!

When you have an idea,
come up with a name and a
logo for your new product.
Draw your logo here.

DESIGN A ROBOT HELPER

Think about the things you have to do that are reeeaaallly boring.
Cleaning your bedroom? Brushing your teeth? Picking up your own mess?

Imagine if you had a robot to do all the boring things for you...

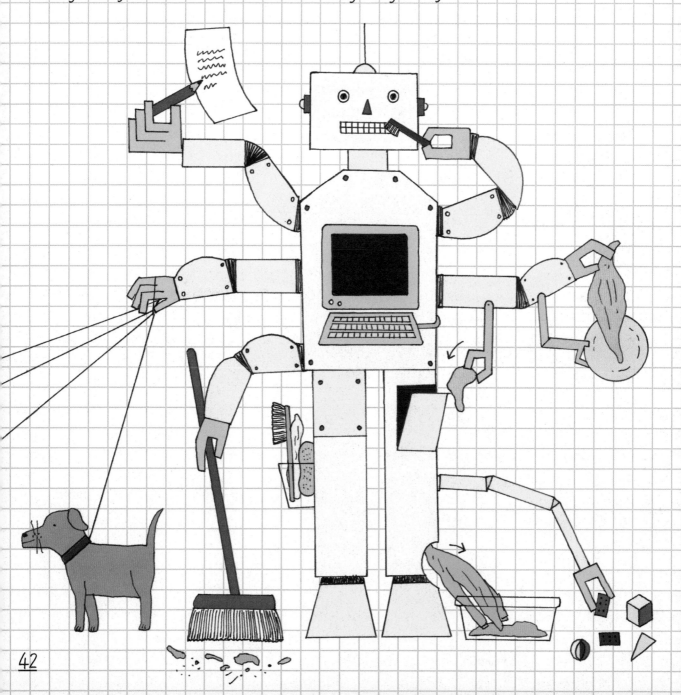

INGENIOUS INVENTIONS

Robots are very useful things.
They can do repetitive, boring
jobs that people don't want to do.
They can also do jobs that would
be too dangerous for a human,
such as going into a building
that might have a bomb inside,
or even exploring other planets.

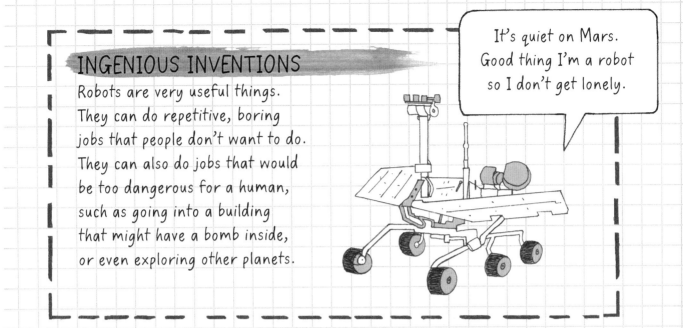

It's quiet on Mars.
Good thing I'm a robot
so I don't get lonely.

DO THIS!

Draw a robot that can help you do
the things you really DON'T LIKE doing.
Add labels to your picture.

FOLLOW EXACT INSTRUCTIONS

Do you know how to make a sandwich? Are you SURE? Below are all the steps involved in making a jam sandwich. But they've been mixed up!

DO THIS!

1st

Read through the steps. Figure out which order they should be in. Write the letters in the correct order for making a jam sandwich in the code box on the opposite page.

A. Take a second slice of bread and press the two slices together so that the jam is between them

B. Take the knife with jam on out of the jar and run the jammy blade across the flat side of a slice of bread

INGENIOUS INVENTIONS

Computers, robots and artificial intelligence work by following algorithms. These are sets of exact instructions written by coders that tell the computer what to do. They have to be very clear because computers aren't like humans who can use background knowledge to help them understand tricky instructions.

C. Pick up the knife and hold it by the handle

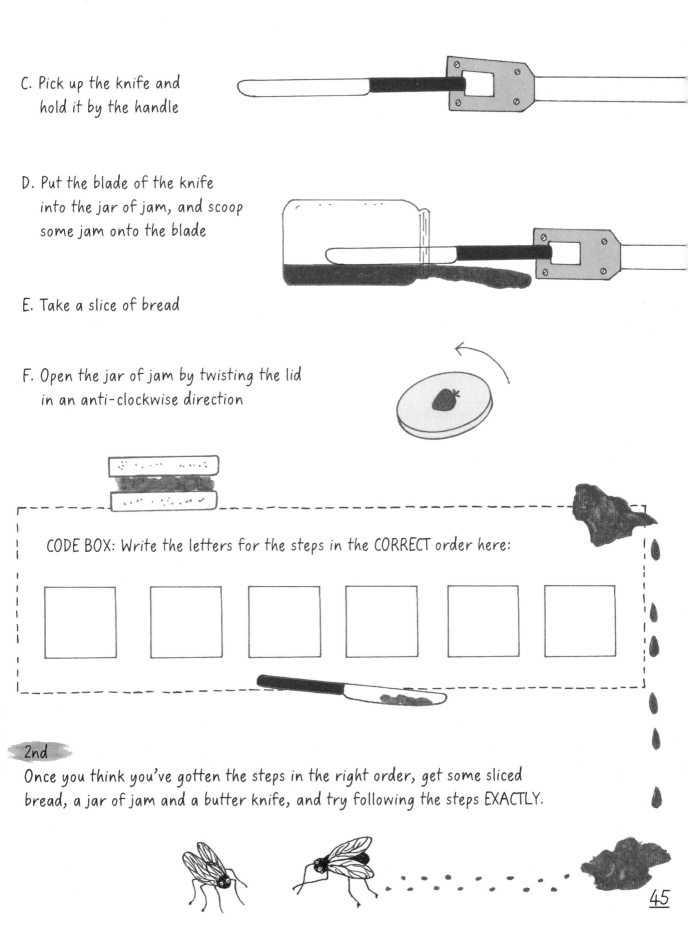

D. Put the blade of the knife into the jar of jam, and scoop some jam onto the blade

E. Take a slice of bread

F. Open the jar of jam by twisting the lid in an anti-clockwise direction

CODE BOX: Write the letters for the steps in the CORRECT order here:

2nd

Once you think you've gotten the steps in the right order, get some sliced bread, a jar of jam and a butter knife, and try following the steps EXACTLY.

THINK LIKE A ROBOT

When you made a jam sandwich on the previous page, you probably already knew what to do without really following the steps. But what if, like a computer, you didn't have any background knowledge? Could you get a task done correctly? It's much harder when you don't already know what to do.

DO THIS!

Turn to page 75 to find some grid paper to draw on, then follow these exact instructions.

1. Draw a 6cm x 6cm square in the middle of the frame.

2. Draw a 2cm x 2cm square above the first box in the center, so the bottom edge of the small square touches the top edge of the big square.

3. Inside the small square draw two dots about 1cm apart. The dots should be lined up horizontally in the middle of the square.

4. On top of the small square, draw a V shape about 2cm tall, with the V's point touching the top edge of the small square.

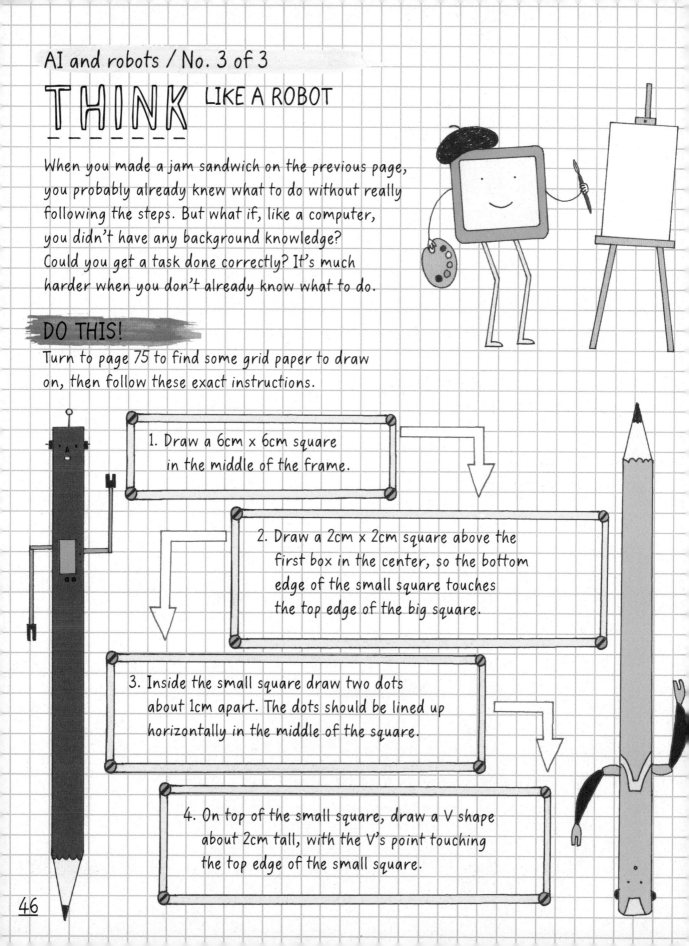

5. Draw two lines below the middle of the big square. The lines should be parallel to one another, 4cm long and 2 cm apart. The top of the lines should meet the bottom edge of the square and run straight downwards from there.

6. On the righthand side of the big square, about 1cm from the top draw a straight line that angles diagonally upward towards the top right corner of the drawing frame, around 3cm long.

7. On the left hand side of the big square, draw another 3cm diagonal line going up towards the top left corner of the drawing frame, so it's like a mirror image of the one on the right hand side.

8. At the ends of the two diagonal lines, draw a capital "C" shape, so that the middle of the C's curve is touching the end of the diagonal line, and the C's tips are facing upward and outward. FINISHED! Now compare your drawing to the original on page 96.

If only I had some instructions for how to eat this.

DO THIS!
Now ask a friend to write some instructions like these for a different drawing. Draw it in the box on page 76. You must follow their instructions EXACTLY—so if their instructions are unclear, don't help them by using your previous knowledge to to draw what they want you to draw!

MAKE A STRUCTURE OUT OF PEOPLE

If you were building a tall structure, what would you make it out of? Perhaps wood, or metal or concrete?

How about people?

Every 2 years in Spain, a competition is held to build the biggest human tower. They are called "castells", meaning "castles". They can be up to 10 tiers high and involve as many as 800 people to build!

Most of the people are in the base of the tower, providing strength and stability for others who climb onto their shoulders. The "crown", or top tier, is usually a small child, around 4 or 5 years old.

TIER 4

I can see my house from here!

Can someone scratch my nose?

TIER 3

TIER 2

TIER 1

DO THIS!

With a few friends, think about what structure you could make just using yourselves. It doesn't have to be tall. You could make a fan-shaped structure:

Or a pyramid-shaped structure...

Or... THE HUMAN TABLE!

1st
Place 4 chairs in a square, each facing inwards like so:

2nd
Invite your friends to sit on the chairs and then all swivel around to their right so they are sitting sideways on the chairs. Ask them to lie back until their shoulders and heads are on the knees of the person behind them.

3rd
Remove the chairs one by one.

Ta-da!
The Human Table!

MEGA WARNING:
Be very careful when making your structure! Make sure you have a lot of space around you and a soft landing. Don't try to stand upright on anyone's shoulders—kneel or sit instead. Focus on cool shapes instead of height.

Don't leave them hanging too long! Replace the chairs after about 1 minute so they can sit up again.

49

BUILD A PAPER SKYSCRAPER

Which skyscraper would you like to live in?

Perhaps you'd like to live in the tallest skyscraper in the world...the Burj Khalifa in Dubai, which is 2,176 ft tall.

Or a horseshoe-shaped building like the Sheraton Hotel in Huzhou, China?

How about an elephant-shaped skyscraper like this one in Thailand?

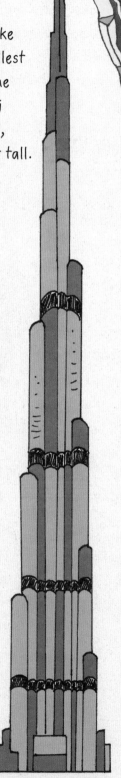

DO THIS!

1st

Make a small model, using paper, of the kind of
skyscraper that you would like to live in. Give yourself
5 minutes to complete it. Try to make it without any tape
or glue—just paper and scissors. GO!

2nd

Now for a real challenge. Get 20 8 ½ x 11 in. sheets of
paper and some sticky tape. What is the tallest paper
skyscraper that you can build that will stand up by itself?
Is it stable enough to be measured? Sketch out
some ideas in the box below before you start.

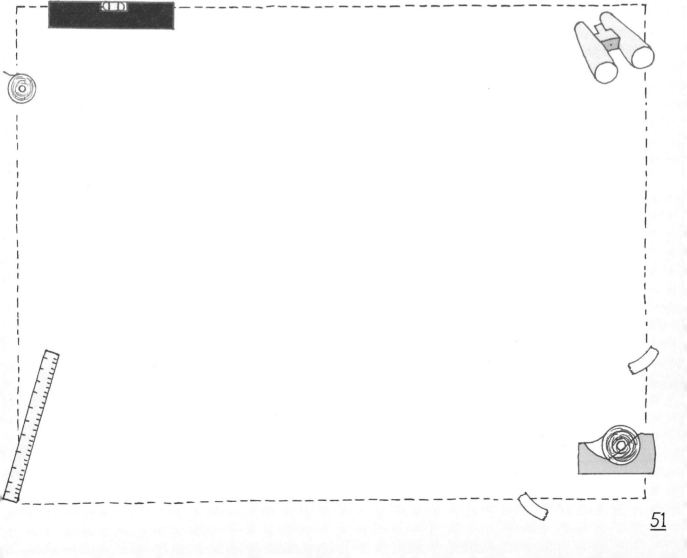

TINKER WITH BRIDGES

Try messing around with some bridges.

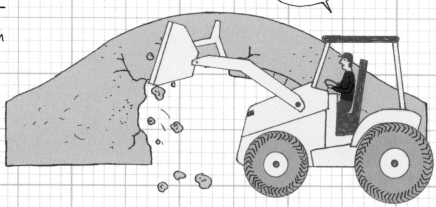

Not REAL bridges of course! Even if you somehow got the cranes and diggers and whatever else you needed to reshape and rebuild some real bridges, it would be illegal. So let's stick to paper, for now.

DO THIS!

Your challenge is to tinker with different bridge designs to test which one is the strongest. Go to page 77 to find the designs.

1st   Place 2 even stacks of books about 6 in apart.

2nd   Fold the 3 pieces of paper from pages 78–82 as instructed.

3rd   One at a time, place each paper bridge on top of the book stacks so it spans the distance between them.

4th   Test how strong each bridge is by placing 1 penny coin on the deck of the bridge (the part you walk on) until it collapses. The bridge that holds the most coins is the strongest.

5th   Test them again with the books only 2 in. apart. How much more can the bridges hold?

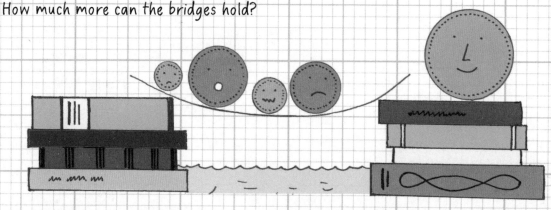

DO THIS!

Document your findings:
Which bridge WINS?!

STRONGEST
BRIDGE
EVER!

Bridge structure	$$$$ on 6 in. span	$$$$ on 2 in. span
Folded		
Tray		
Triangle		

INGENIOUS INVENTIONS

A suspension bridge is a type of bridge where the deck is hung from cables. The cables are suspended between towers and anchored at each end of the bridge. The longest suspension bridge in the world is the Akashi-Kaikyo Bridge in Japan. The middle span is 6,532 ft..

GET WIND (TO POWER A MACHINE)

Have you got wind? It's really great. You see, wind can be used to generate electricity without needing to burn oil or gas, which cause global warming.

My wrist hurts!

Electricity can be generated by spinning magnets very fast inside coils of wire. But how do you spin the big, heavy magnets fast enough to generate an electric current?

Simple! You use a turbine. A turbine is basically a big fan that spins round, pushed by a current of air (or water or steam). The turbines spin the magnets inside to generate the electricity.

I love wind turbines. I'm a big fan of big fans.

Traditional power stations burn oil or gas in order to boil water. The boiling water makes jets of steam that spin big turbines. But burning oil or gas releases greenhouse gases into the air, which trap the sun's heat and cause climate change. So why not cut out that part and just use air that is already moving—the wind!

DO THIS!

Build a windmill that uses the wind power from a hairdryer to lift a small amount of weight, such as a paper cup with coins inside. Think about the size, thickness and number of blades your windmill has. Improve your design as you make it.

If you're feeling stuck, how about designing something like this:

paper strip

fan blades

tape

string with weight

SAVE THE WORLD

A long time ago, a singer named Whitney Houston said "I believe the children are our future." And considering what a mess grown-ups have made of the planet, with climate change, plastic pollution and all the rest, she probably had a point! Luckily, there are young people all over the world thinking of clever ways to solve the problems that adults have caused.

The earth-saving super teens

After learning that her friend in the Philippines didn't have reliable electricity or light to be able to study, Ann Makosinski invented a torch that runs off the heat from your hand. She was 14.

When she was 17, Cynthia Sin Nga Lam invented a portable device that purifies water and produces electricity at the same time. Neat!

Param Jaggi was 17 when he invented a tube to place over car exhaust pipes that uses algae to turn carbon dioxide (a greenhouse gas) into harmless oxygen and sugar.

DO THIS!

What do you see as the biggest problems facing the world right now?
Imagine, draw and label your inventions for solving them in the boxes below.

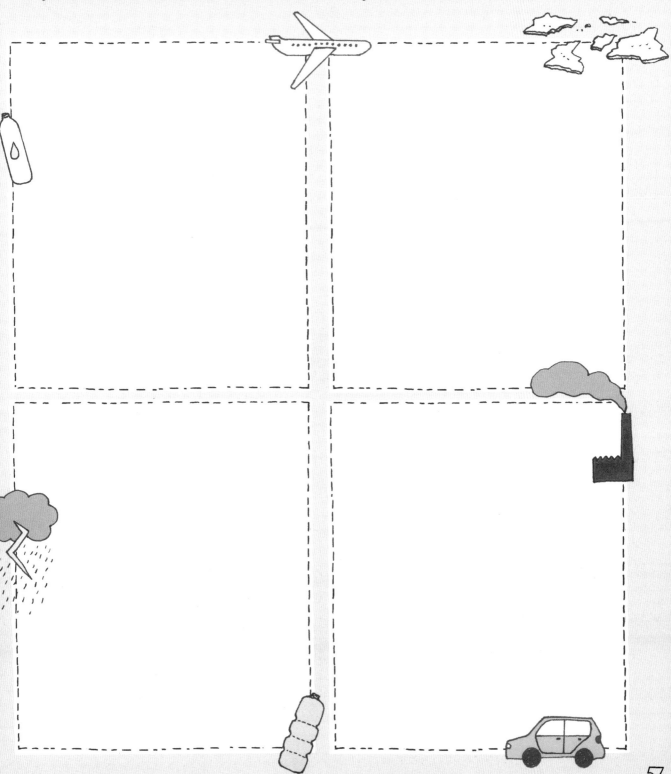

READ WITHOUT LOOKING

How do you read a book without your eyes?
Answer: you use your hands.

In 1824, 15-year-old Louis Braille created the
Braille alphabet, a system that uses raised
dots to show letters and sounds.
A blind person can read
by running their fingertips
over the dots.

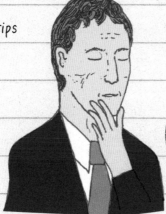

In Braille, the dots are arranged within rectangular grids called "cells."
Each cell contains six possible dot positions in two columns of three rows.
For example, in English Braille, the letters A and Z look like this:

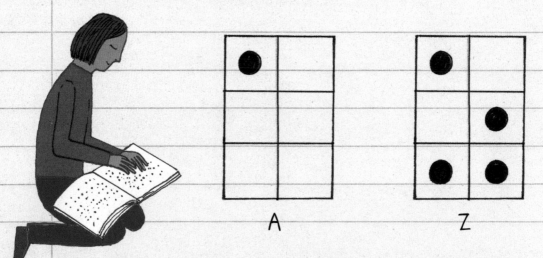

DO THIS!

Plan a message to send to a friend in Braille.

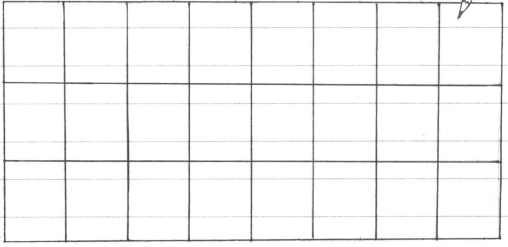

1st

Plan what you want your (short) message to your friend to say, and write it in this box:

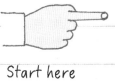

Start here

2nd

Now REWRITE the same message, but BACKWARDS, so that the first letter of the first word is on the far right of the page. For example, if you wrote "Hello pal," you would write it like this: "lap olleH."

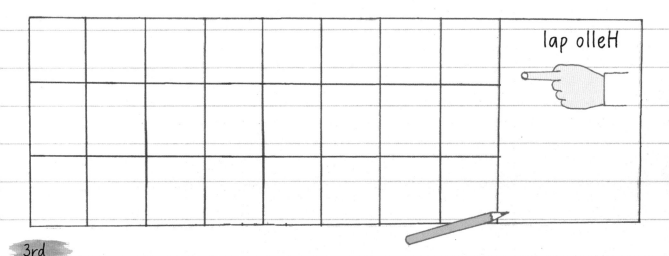

lap olleH

3rd

Now turn to page 83 to find the stencil that will help you translate your message into Braille!

FIGHT OFF THE PLASTIC ATTACK!

Eek!

Do you ever feel like you just can't escape plastic?

Plastic doesn't rot, but most of it isn't recycled either, so our plastic usage creates vast amounts of trash that piles up on land, or escapes into the ocean.

In the ocean, animals swallow plastic trash, causing them to get sick and die. Fish and other creatures get caught in the floating trash, also killing them. It's bad news!

I don't feel so good...

But once again, it's kids and teens who are leading the way in developing inventions to solve the problem of plastic pollution...

BANANA PLASTIC

What if you could make plastic that biodegrades, or breaks down, just like plants do? Ask 16-year-old Elif Bilgin! She was troubled by the amount of plastic pollution in her home city of Istanbul in Turkey.

Elif found a way to make plastic by pureeing banana peels, mixing them with chemicals and baking the mixture. The result is a strong, hard plastic material that rots like a plant.

OCEAN CLEANUP

What about all the plastic that's already in the ocean? At age 16, Boyan Slat began developing a system of floating trash collectors that could collect all the plastic floating in the ocean. He thinks that they could clear up to 90% of the Great Pacific Garbage Patch (a huge area of floating plastic) by 2040. Each collector has a "skirt" attached to a flotation device that slowly gathers up trash as it drifts on ocean currents.

DO THIS!

Brilliant ideas like this can only save the world if they are widely put into action. Go to page 87 to learn how to ADVERTISE your plastic-busting idea!

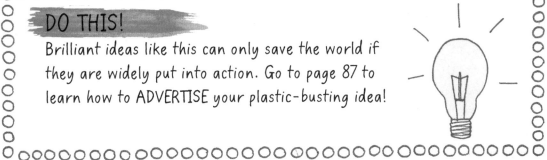

THIS BOOK THINKS IT'S A TINKERING SPACE

This section of the book contains pages for you to cut out, cut up, fold and stick.

THE WHEEL OF INVENTION

DO THIS!

Cut this wheel out and poke a pencil through the middle of the circle to turn it into a spinner. Use it to spin the wheel of invention on page 12.

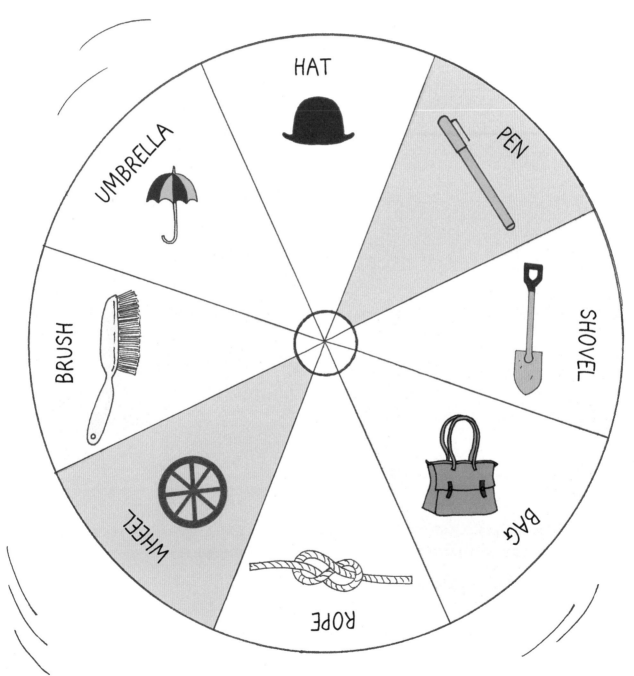

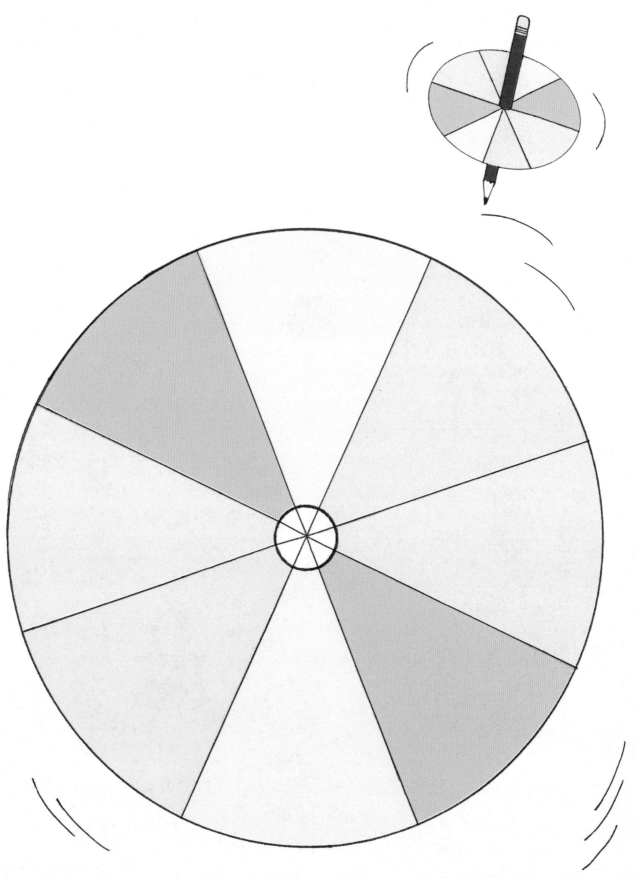

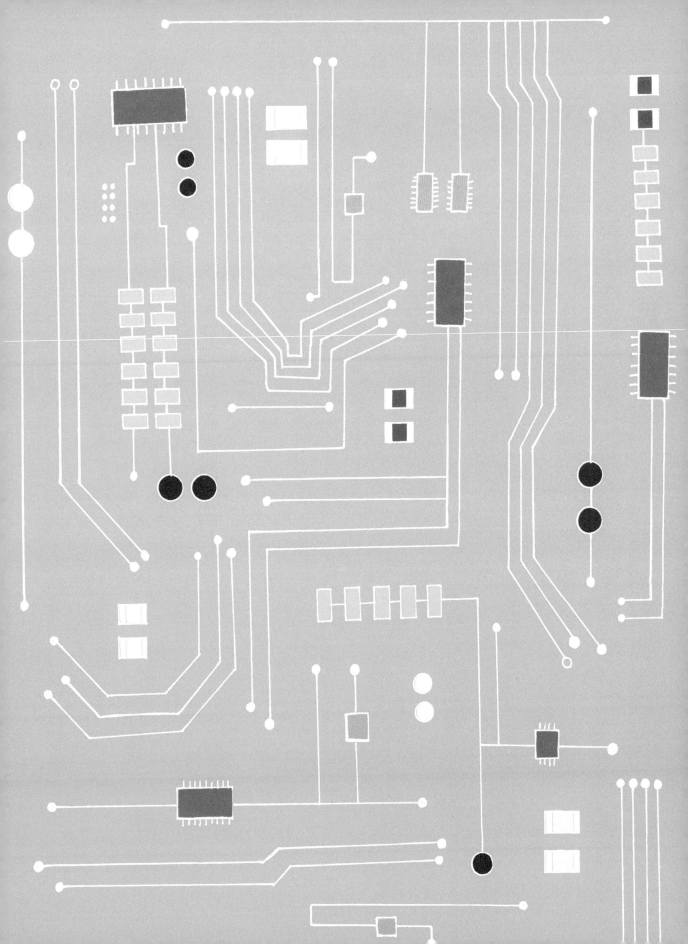

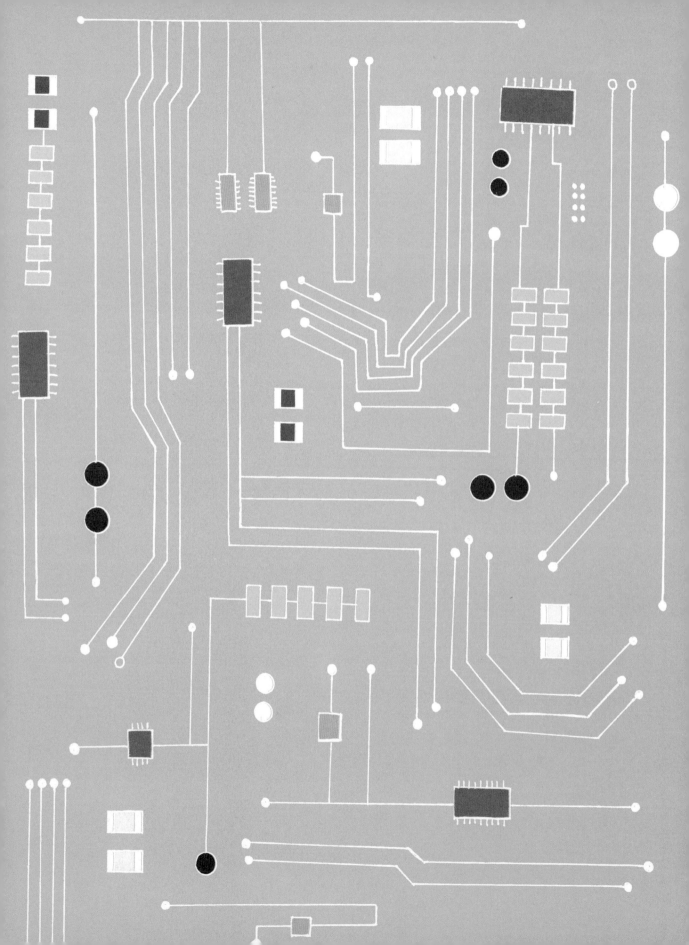

PING YOUR PRINCE PIECES

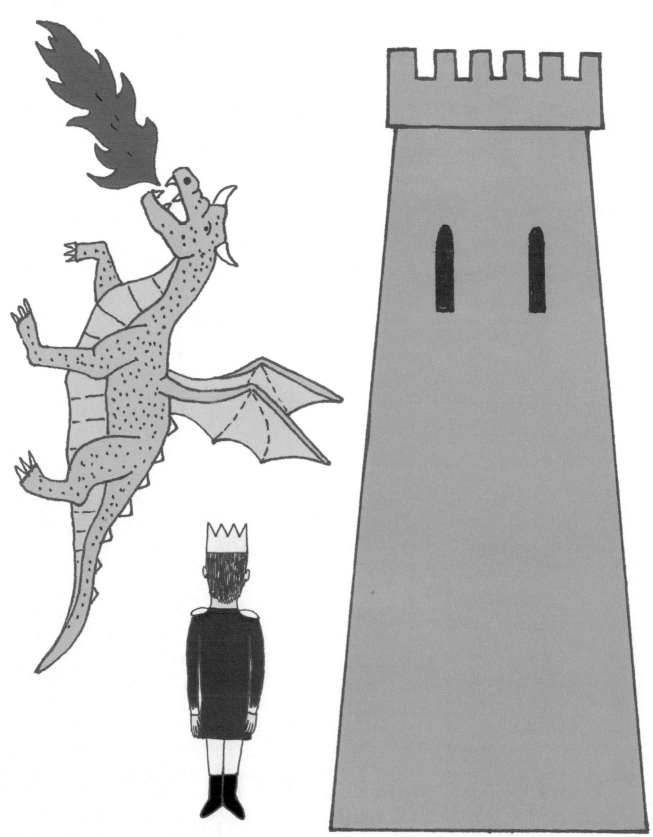

PAPER FLYING MACHINES

DO THIS!

Make a paper hoop glider and a paper helicopter. You'll need scissors, a paper clip, tape and a drinking straw.

Paper hoop glider

1st

Cut out the two colored strips at the side of this page. Curl them into circles, and tape them at either end of your drinking straw so they look like this:

2nd

Throw your hoop glider from a high place and watch it go!

Paper helicopter

1st

Cut out the paper helicopter template on the opposite page. Cut along the dotted lines and fold along the solid lines. Fold the sides of the body in to make it narrower and thicker.

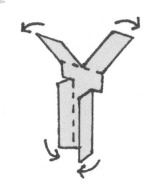

2nd

Fold the bottom part of the body up and put a paper clip on it for weight. Fold the top wings in opposite directions.

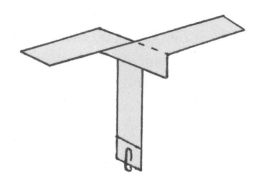

3rd

Drop the paper helicopter from a height and watch it twirl. There are 2 templates, so why not challenge a friend or sibiling?

PAPER HELICOPTER PIECES

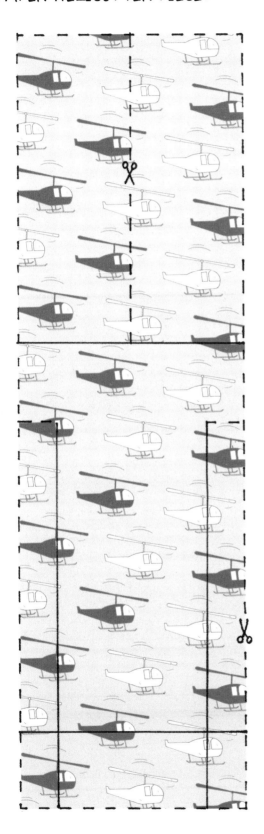

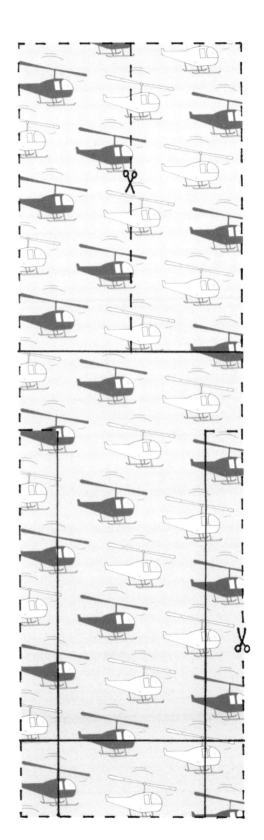

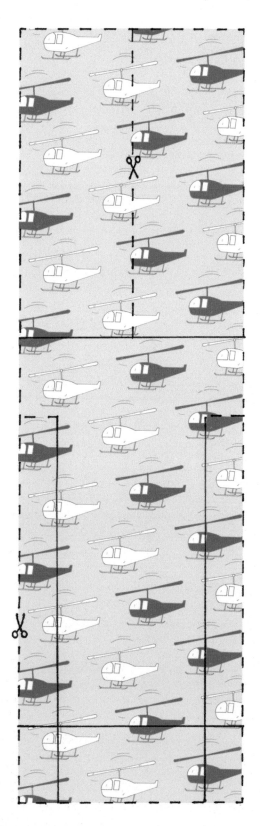
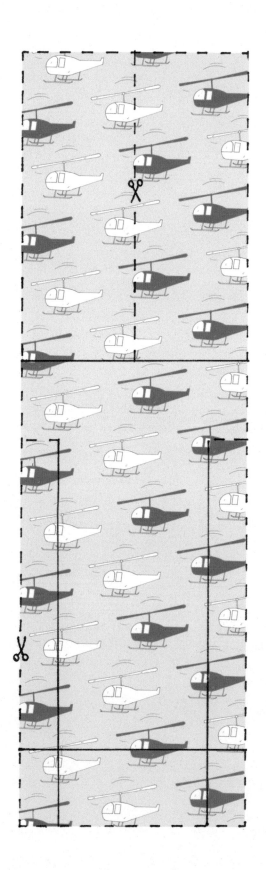

THINK LIKE A ROBOT

DO THIS!

Follow the steps from page 46 to create an image in the picture frame below.

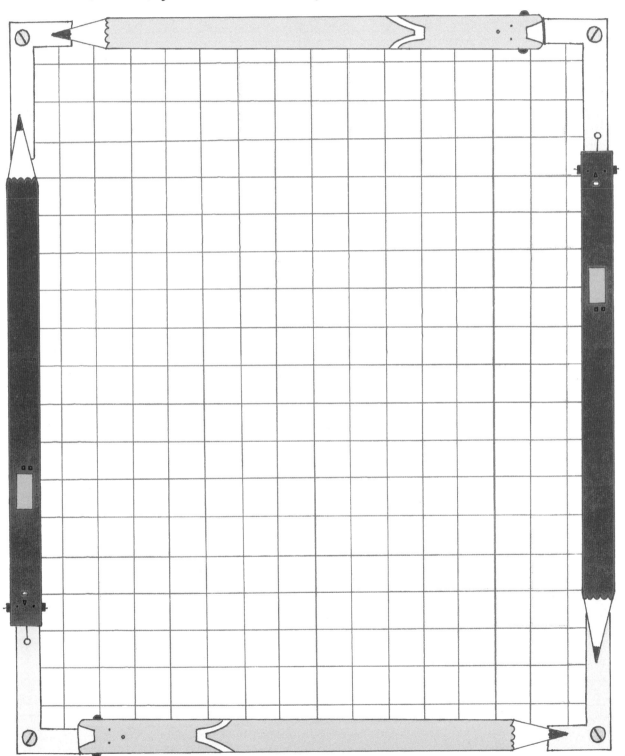

DO THIS!

Use this space to draw whatever your friend instructs you to.

TINKER WITH BRIDGES

DO THIS!

Use the next three pages to complete the paper
bridge challenge on page 52. Which bridge will win?

The folded bridge?

The tray bridge?

The triangle bridge?

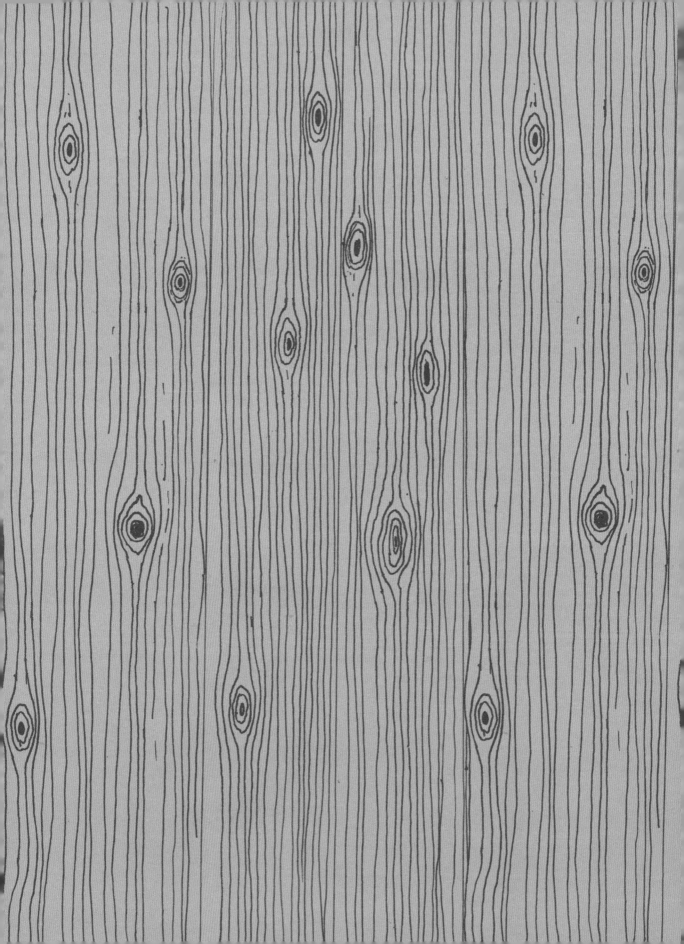

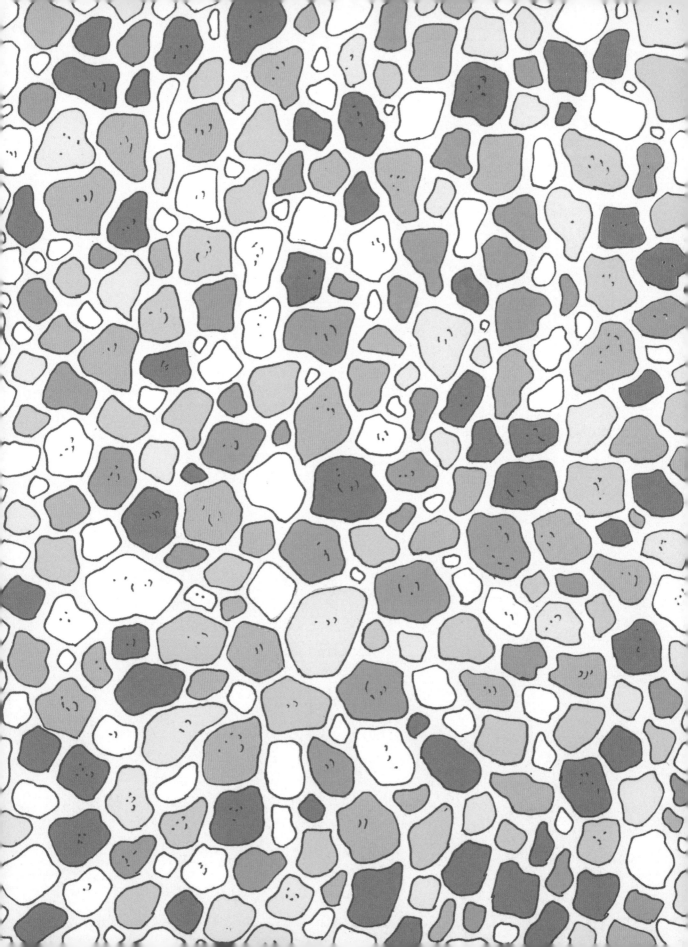

READ WITHOUT LOOKING

DO THIS!

First, plan a message to send to a friend in Braille on p59.
Next, translate your message into raised Braille dots.
YOU WILL NEED: a lump of modeling clay, a sharp pencil,
and a loose piece of note paper.

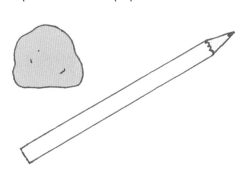

1st

Squash the modeling clay flat and place your
piece of note paper on top of it. Place the
Braille STENCIL on top of that, with the blue side
facing upwards.

blue Braille STENCIL
this side up

note paper

modeling clay

2nd

Look at the message that you wrote
BACKWARDS on page 59. Find the first Braille
letter in your message on the stencil and line it
up with the top right corner of your note paper.

3rd

Punch holes through the black dots that make up the first Braille letter of your message. Make sure you punch right through the stencil, the note paper and into the modeling clay. Punch out one letter at a time, moving the stencil around to create the rest of the letters that make up your message.

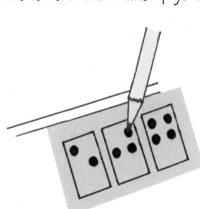

4th

Once you have punched out your full message, put the Braille stencil aside. Carefully peel the note paper off the modeling clay, turn the page over and feel the raised Braille dots that have been created.

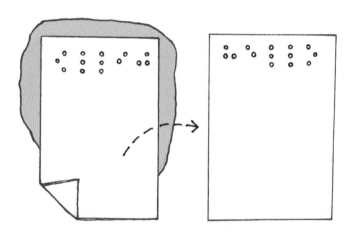

5th

Find an envelope. Inside it place your note paper with its Braille message, along with the RED Braille alphabet sheet from p85. Send the envelope to your friend for them decode your Braille message.

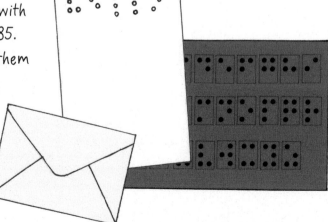

BRAILLE ALPHABET SHEET Decode the Braille message using this sheet.

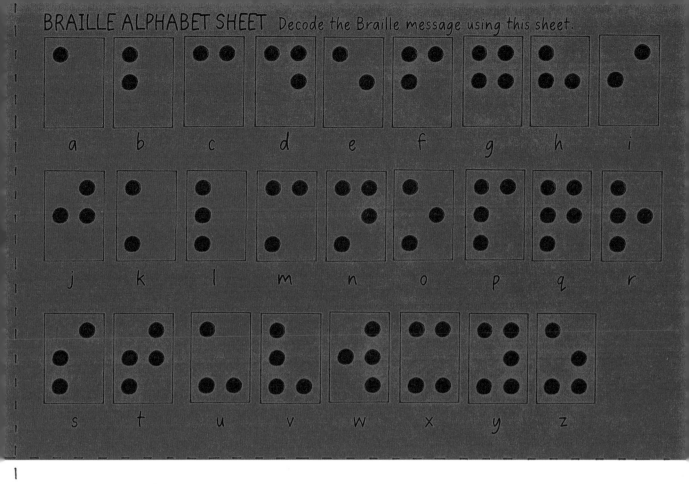

Cut along the dotted lines to remove this RED Braille alphabet sheet from the book. Include the alphabet sheet in the envelope with your Braille message as instructed on p84.

Turn over the page to discover the BLUE Braille stencil which you will need for making raised Braille letters.

Dear Friend,

This Braille alphabet sheet was invented to help you decode my message which is written entirely using raised Braille dots. Each arrangement of raised dots represents a different letter of the alphabet. Can you decode my message?

Yours sincerely,

....

STAY SHARP WITH THIS BRAILLE DECODER!

BRAILLE STENCIL
Place the stencil this side up against your note paper.

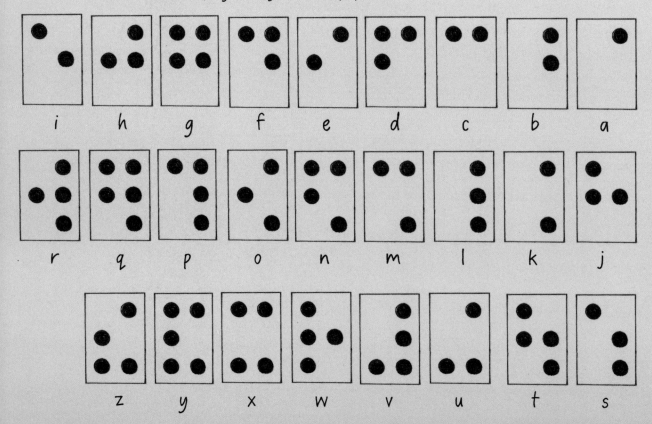

FIGHT OFF THE PLASTIC ATTACK!

DO THIS!

Use the next few pages to design, patent, advertise and sell an invention that can help solve the plastic pollution crisis. It could be a way to clean up plastic waste, or find a new use for it, or an invention that replaces plastic objects with ones less harmful to the environment.

1st

Use this space for your research. What are the problems? What other inventions exist that also try to solve the problem? How do they work?

Hmmm, can pollution be bottled up?

In this box, draw and label your invention.
You could draw it from more than one angle, if you like.

3rd

Apply for a patent. When an inventor invents something new, they can apply to the government for a patent. This stops other people from making or selling the same invention without the inventor's permission for a set period of time. Fill out the Patent Application Form below.

NAME OF INVENTION _____

_____

NAME OF INVENTOR _____

CURRENT STATE OF THE ART
(in this section you list any similar inventions that already exist)

_____

_____

_____

DESCRIPTION OF INVENTION WITH DIAGRAM

Advertise your invention. Think about the ads you see for products on posters at the bus stop or on billboards. Design one for your invention. You might want to come up with a slogan, or tag-line, but try not to have too many words on the ad. Instead, think about how you can use a picture to convey what it is, why it's so great, and why people should buy it. Draw your poster here.

DID YOU KNOW

Thomas Edison is famous for inventing the lightbulb. But British inventor Joseph Swan invented the lightbulb first and Edison, um, "developed" (that is, he copied) Swan's idea. So why do we remember Edison, not Swan? Because Edison was better at advertising his invention!

Finally, when your product is ready to go on sale, you'll need to write an instruction booklet to go with it.
What are the possible uses of your invention? How does it work?
Cut out and fold the page below into a booklet shape, and write the instruction manual for your invention, including steps for assembling any parts.

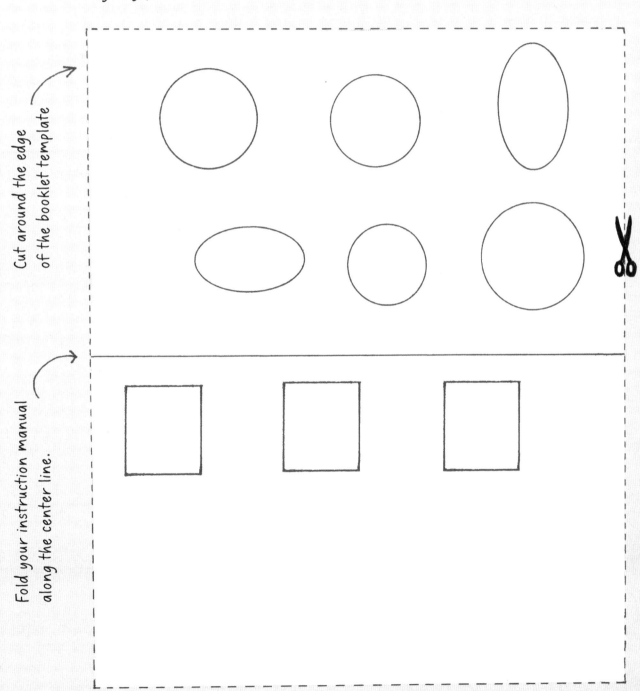

Cut around the edge of the booklet template

Fold your instruction manual along the center line.

This is what your instruction manual should look like!

INSTRUCTIONS FOR ....

Designed by ....
Age ....

DOODLE INVENTIONS

On these pages, the beginnings of some possible inventions have been drawn for you. Finish these doodly inventions by turning them into whatever wacky contraptions you want. Give them a name and label the important parts.

ANSWERS

Page 38

A) a pager from 1985. A pager is a machine that can receive text messages, but nothing else. If someone wanted to send you a message on your pager, they called an operator on the telephone and told them the message. The operator typed it and sent it to your pager. They are still used by emergency services because the signal is more reliable than cell phones.

B) a 1920s toaster.

C) a washing machine and mangle from 1897. The clothes were put in the tub with water and spun around by turning the handle on the side. The wet washing was then put through the rollers at the top to squeeze the water out.

D) a personal stereo cassette player (for listening to music) from 1998.

Page 46

Correct drawing from exact instructions challenge

GOODBYE